Reflections

Daily messages for finding strength
in difficult times

DEANNA KAHLER

Forward

I collapsed into a sobbing heap on the staircase in our two-story home. The familiar pain pierced through my heart and tugged at my soul. Miscarriage was a sadness I never expected to experience—and certainly not twice. But here I was again. Heartbroken...devastated...uncertain of what the future held...unsure of how I would carry on.

She may not have been born or even fully developed, but this was my child, my baby. She had died inside of me before even being given a chance to live. My hopes and dreams of becoming a mom were shattered that day. And in the months that followed, a part of me blamed myself. I felt guilty that my body couldn't do what it was designed to do: carry a baby to term. I grieved deeply for the children I never met or held in my arms.

The year was 2002. Little did I know: I would go on to adopt a beautiful baby girl and write a book to help countless women cope with their own miscarriages and navigate the often over-whelming adoption process. I found writing to be very healing and also loved that I could share my experiences to help others.

Fast forward to 2022. I found myself in a courtroom with the person who was supposed to be my partner for life. We had spent 34 years together, 27 of them married. We met and fell in love at age 19, still kids but convinced we were ready to be adults. We shared many laughs and tears, and most of all, so much love. But over the years, resentment built, misunderstandings happened, arguments ensued and betrayal tore us apart. Now we stood next to each other with our attorneys, prepared to sever our bond as a couple.

Before approving our divorce, the judge asked if there was anything anyone wanted to say. My husband's attorney spoke:

"Your honor, I just want to commend both parties for the way they handled everything. It was refreshing to have a case where the couple didn't have a lot of debt, got along well and worked together. A case like this is very rare."

My husband—who normally has difficulty expressing emotions—began to cry.

"I'm sad it didn't work out," he sobbed.

I had been fighting back tears myself and could no longer contain them. My attorney reached out and put her hand on my back to comfort me. Even the judge got teary-eyed.

Still, the divorce went on. After leaving the courtroom, both attorneys reminded us that we didn't have to do this. But we did. As hard as it was, we both knew our relationship was over.

I felt like someone died that day. I left the courtroom a lonely, heartbroken woman. Months later, I'm still lonely and broken, although a little less so. I sometimes long for what once was. I miss my intact family. I miss the love my ex and I once shared. I miss the happier days. Sometimes,

I still cry for what I've lost. Other days, I want to stay in bed and block out the world. Most of the time, I keep busy and keep living, despite how I am feeling.

Grief really sucks. When it strikes, you lose a part of yourself and are never the same again. You must somehow learn to carry on, to find a new path and a new way of living. You don't have a choice. You're powerless over the situation. As much as you wish you could go back and change things, you can't. Such is the case with any loss, life challenge or trauma. That's where this book comes in.

Over the years, I've used reading and writing to heal, and now I'd like to pass some of that along to you. This work is a culmination of my life experiences. I've certainly had my share of challenges—health, family, relationships and career. Along with miscarriages and divorce, I've suffered from autoimmune and heart issues, anxiety and panic attacks. I was in an abusive relationship as a teenager. My daughter has life-threatening food allergies and struggles with mental health issues, which has been scary and overwhelming for both her and our family. It's all a lot to deal with!

I'll admit some days I didn't know how I would get through any of it. The truth is: I'm *still* healing. But what I've done before and what I'm doing again is using my experiences and the insight I've gained to help others.

Rather than write a book about mental health or divorce or grief, I opted for a little guide with messages to help you get through your own challenges. Many of these thoughts came to me during some of my darkest times, and somehow helped me find a way to carry on in the midst of incredible pain and sadness. I hope that as you read the words and look at the inspirational photos from my personal collection, you will feel a little less alone and a little more empowered to face another day and move forward with your life.

Sending peace, love and healing to you on your journey!

Warmly,
Deanna Kahler

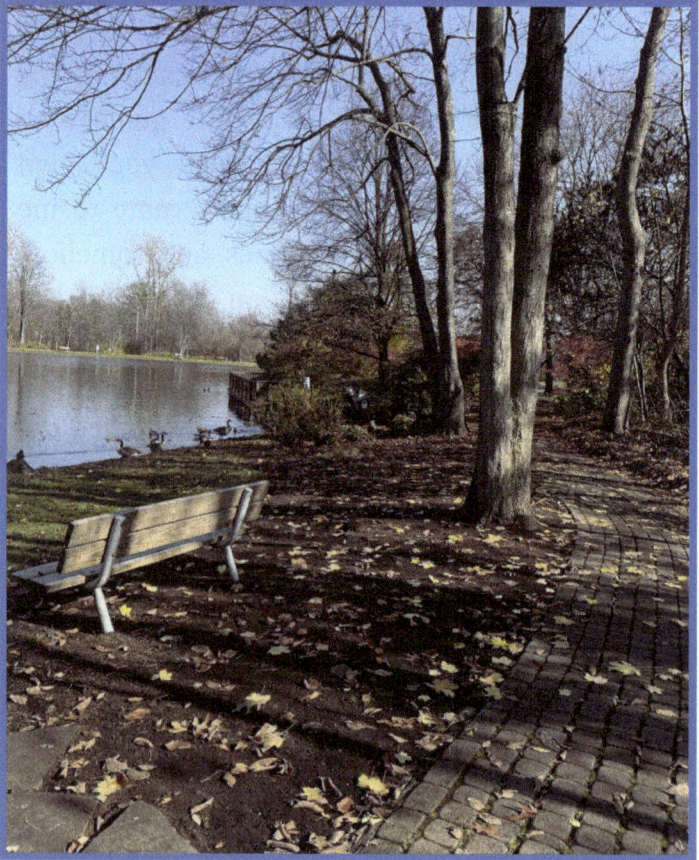

Day 1

Healing takes time

I can't do this. I just want the pain to end. It's unbearable. Sound familiar?

When we suffer a loss or experience trauma, the pain we feel can be excruciating. You may wonder how you will ever get through it.

When I lost my first baby, my life spiraled into a world of sadness, devastation and anxiety. I remember describing it as a black hole I had fallen into and could not get out of. I felt so alone, like no one understood and no one could help me. I just wanted it all to end.

It's natural to want to get through the pain as quickly as possible. No one wants to feel horrible or suffer. But unfortunately, that's not how healing works. Healing doesn't take place quickly, but rather over a long period of time. Little by little, bit by bit, each day we heal.

Depending on the circumstances, it may take weeks, months or even many years. In some cases, we never fully heal, but instead get to a place where we recover enough to go on with our lives.

Relief is not immediate because healing is a process. Try not to pressure yourself to get through something before you're ready. And whatever you do, please don't short circuit your healing process by numbing your pain or filling the void with alcohol, drugs, gambling, shopping, sex or premature new relationships. You may feel some temporary relief, but you're really only delaying the healing process. Nothing or no one can speed that up for you. The only way through grief is to experience it.

Allow yourself all the time you need to process your emotions, grieve your losses and eventually heal.

+ + +

Day 2

The human soul is unbreakable

Like many of you, I've felt totally defeated during some of the most difficult times in my life. As humans, we often feel this way when faced with hardships, losses or challenges. It's unfortunately part of the human experience. What we sometimes forget, however, is that nothing can truly break our souls. That is where our strength lies.

A conversation with my mom recently got me thinking about this very point. To help you understand, I'll share our text conversation:

Mom: We're very worried about you.
Me: I'm fine. Don't worry.
Mom: No, you're not. I'm your mother.
Me: No, really I am.
Mom: Don't lie to me. How can u be fine after all that?
Me: Because I'm a survivor

Enough said.

I'm a survivor, and so are you. We may be hurting or in pain...our bodies may grow weary...our hearts may be broken, but our souls are always intact, ready to carry us forward wherever our journeys may lead.

People can hurt you. Life can test you. However, nothing can destroy you. Despite everything that has ever happened or ever will happen, you are a survivor. The fact that you are still here today is proof of that.

✦ ✦ ✦

Day 3

Your joy is on the other side of pain

As I walked through my neighborhood one day and thought about what it takes to be happy, this phrase came to mind: *Your joy is on the other side of pain.*

We've all had painful and traumatic experiences that interfere with our lives and hold us back. I've spent a lot of time wishing life could be the way it used to be. Like many of you, I've tried hard to somehow get back what was lost and have resisted what is. This does nothing but keep us stuck!

Getting through the pain first involves ACCEPT-ANCE. You finally say to yourself: This is the way my life is right now. There is no going back.

To find joy again, we need to take on the pain and fully experience it before we can move on. Cry, scream, get angry, write in a journal, talk to a trusted friend—do whatever you need to do to work through that pain.

Don't fight against it, pretend it's not there or try to make it go away. Instead, travel through it. It won't be easy, but when you emerge on the other side, you will be able to find happiness again.

+ + +

Day 4

Help is never far away

Have you ever felt conflicted, sad or confused about something and then suddenly noticed signs that point you in the right direction? You're not alone. Some people call them "God-winks;" others use the term "synchronicity." But no matter what you choose to call these events, they remind us that there is a much larger force at work in our lives.

What we sometimes forget during our busy schedules is that we can ask for and seek guidance at any time. We don't have to muddle through life alone, nor do we have to carry the weight of the world on our shoulders. Simply ask and you shall receive.

This doesn't mean you'll always get the answer you were hoping for, but you will get the support and guidance you need.

When a loved one had cancer, I was terrified of losing her. It was very difficult to watch her suffer and grow weaker each day. I felt powerless to help her, although I tried. At one point, I even questioned whether or not she would survive. I voiced my concerns in a silent prayer and asked for God's help.

That week, I saw not one but *three* rainbows! Never before had I witnessed so many rainbows in such a short period of time. Because of this miraculous occurrence, I knew in my heart that my prayers were being answered and she would be okay. Today, she is healthy, thriving and cancer-free.

Those rainbows spoke to me in a way that no person on earth could. They urged me to have hope and to keep the faith at a time when life seemed so uncertain and out of control. I needed some comfort and reassurance—and I received it.

Not every story in our lives has a happy ending like this one. But no matter what challenges, hardships or obstacles we face, we can take comfort in knowing we are never truly alone. Help, comfort or guidance is always a simple prayer away.

Next time you are feeling depressed, afraid, uncertain or conflicted, try asking for your own sign or guidance. You just may be surprised at what comes your way!

✛ ✛ ✛

Day 5

This too shall pass

Throughout my life, whenever I was faced with a challenge or hardship, my mother would remind me: "This too shall pass." This simple yet powerful phrase has helped to carry me through some of my toughest times.

When we're in the midst of a struggle, it can be difficult to see the light at the end of the tunnel. We may not see any signs of relief, so we feel like we'll be trapped in our current situation forever. But life is dynamic—it's in a constant state of change. As hard as it is right now, whatever you're dealing with will eventually come to pass. You will get through it. Hang in there and have faith that better days are ahead. And remember what I said before: You are never alone. To help further illustrate my point, I'll share another example of Divine intervention:

When my husband was in the hospital several years ago, I was very worried. After a difficult day, I left the hospital late that night to head home to my young daughter. I had been holding back my own emotions for hours, in an attempt to be strong for him. As soon as I reached the parking lot, my emotions overcame me. It was dark and quiet, and no one was around, so I burst into tears. I got into my car and sobbed. I felt powerless and afraid. I doubted my ability to get through the situation. I began praying really hard for several minutes, pleading: "Please help me! I don't know if I can do this!" Then I turned on the radio and immediately heard:

"I'll be there for you. These five words I swear to you. When you breathe, I wanna be the air for you. I'll be there for you."

A funny feeling came over me at that moment, and I stopped crying. Those were the very words I needed to hear. A sense of peace and reassurance filled me, and I quickly realized that although I felt completely alone in my car, I wasn't really. God heard my tearful prayers and had answered me.

This difficult time did pass. And with a little help, everyone made it through. You will too.

✦ ✦ ✦

Day 6

Embrace the calm amid the chaos

One morning, I stayed in bed until 9:30 a.m. for the first time in years. I didn't sleep well during the night because my mind was busy thinking and trying to make sense of everything. What I quickly realized is that I probably never will.

Sometimes the world just doesn't make sense. Sometimes things happen that are out of our control, and we must learn to adapt. The world is an uncertain and chaotic place right now. That doesn't mean we can't find moments of calm and peace amid the craziness. Today, I urge you to look for and embrace those moments. Here are some ideas:

Rest – Enjoy a little extra rest like I did that day. I must admit it was nice to actually have a break from all the activities and busyness of life.

Get outside – Studies have shown that being outdoors has many health benefits, including reducing anxiety and depression, relieving fatigue and even decreasing inflammation. Try a nice walk, jog or bike ride to boost your mood and relieve stress.

Connect – Nurture your relationships. Spend some extra time with your loved ones and enjoy the opportunity to strengthen your bonds. Remember what matters most in life—the people you care about.

Take a break from social media – While informative and sometimes entertaining, social media actually increases your anxiety. Reading too many stories about the pandemic, shootings or other disturbing news stories provokes panic and causes us to think irrationally. Be sure to put down your phone or get off your computer for a while each day.

Get creative – Do a craft, art project or some writing. During the height of the Covid-19 pandemic, my daughter made tie-dye shirts and decorated coasters. We also ordered a paint-at-home kit and watched an instructional video to create cool paintings. These activities can be very therapeutic. Do something fun you always wanted to do, but never had time for.

Remember, you won't feel this way forever. Seek out these peaceful moments to help keep you feeling well during times of uncertainty.

✦ ✦ ✦

Day 7

Life is what happens while we're making other plans

After a recent string of bad luck and family challenges, I reflected on what advice I have to share on coping with life's crises.

Life can take some unexpected turns, often when we least expect it. No matter how hard we work, how much we love our family and friends, or how nice we are, bad things can and do happen. I know from personal experience that it's easy to blame yourself when things go wrong. You may wonder: What could I have done differently?

But looking backwards and second-guessing yourself accomplishes nothing. Instead, we must set our sights on the future and learn from our mistakes.

Life is a cycle of unpredictable ups and downs. If you're in a low place right now, take comfort in knowing the cycle will eventually change. You will rise again. Until then, it's okay to not have all the answers. It's alright when things don't work out the way you hoped or planned.

At the time when my marriage was failing and my daughter was struggling with her mental health, I felt a sense of urgency to "fix" things. I worried the problems would get worse if I didn't do something right away. What I forgot was: there is really no rush. We can tackle an issue one step at a time and don't always need to know what we're going to do next. We don't have to have a plan. In fact, sometimes there is really nothing we can do at all. Not every problem is solvable.

I found that out with my marriage. For years, I kept hoping we could "fix" things. We went to couple's therapy and our relationship improved for a while. Then, we found ourselves right back to the way we were. Our relationship was plagued with misunderstandings, resentment, arguments, and disagreements over how to parent. I was trying to heal from my husband's betrayal.

We both felt unloved and unappreciated. We suffered from communication and intimacy issues. Our marriage life was a series of struggles, which resulted in us becoming more like roommates than a couple. I tried hard to come up with a way to make our relationship work. In the end, it was better to just let go and move on instead of staying unhappy and miserable.

It took quite a while to get to the point of filing for divorce. Seven years to be exact. This may seem like a really long time, but remember when faced with a challenge or major life decision, you need to work at your own pace. You don't have to figure everything out right now. Change is a process. It takes time. Allow yourself the time you need to sit with your problems and don't pressure yourself to come up with an ideal solution right away. Sometimes, you need time to sort things out before moving forward.

This is definitely true when coping with the aftermath of a divorce or failed relationship. I have no idea what's next for me. The future is uncertain. At first, I thought I needed to figure out what I want to do. Now, I just get up each day, go to work and take care of my daughter. I realize I don't have to know where my life is headed. I can just live it until I'm ready to make a change or decide what I want to do next.

Maybe my future includes another love interest; maybe it doesn't. All I know right now is that I'm not ready to pursue anything. I still have a lot of healing to do. And that's okay.

✦ ✦ ✦

Day 8

You can't plan everything. Sometimes you have to just wing it

About six years ago, we were all packed and ready to travel from Detroit to St. Louis to visit our friends. We had planned to leave at 7 a.m. on a Friday morning. However, at 3:30 a.m., I heard a strange squeaky noise in our house. I headed down the hallway in the dark and felt a whoosh of flapping wings whisk past me. I flicked on the lights and was horrified to find two bats flying around our great room. This was NOT how our vacation was supposed to start!

We spent most of our day dealing with the situation and were seriously considering canceling our trip. However, by the end of the day, we made a last-minute decision to leave that night and drive part way—with no real plan and no hotel reservations. I'm usually a planner, so this was definitely out of character for me. But it felt like the right thing to do. So we set off at 8 p.m. and finally settled into a hotel at 1 a.m.

The point is: we can do our best to make plans and follow them, but we cannot plan for everything. You just never know what life will throw your way. During these unexpected times, we have a choice. We can throw our hands in the air and feel defeated or we can work with what we have. I'm not typically a spontaneous person, but in the midst of our chaos, making a spur-of-the-moment choice empowered me. It allowed me to rise above the current situation and turn it into a more positive one.

Sometimes the decisions that arise in the moment are some of the most rewarding ones. Don't ever feel like you're locked into a plan. Free yourself to go with the flow and wing it once in a while.

✦ ✦ ✦

Day 9

The answers you seek are within

Sometimes life leaves us feeling confused and wondering what to do. During these times, we often search for answers.

Maybe you call a friend or family member to get their advice. Perhaps you search the internet for articles or tips on how to deal with a situation. This is all good and fine, as long as you remember that you are the only one who knows what is right for you.

Whether you realize it or not, you are your most valuable resource. This is where intuition comes in. We all have that inner voice or gut feeling that tells us whether or not something is right or wrong in our lives.

Have you ever had a feeling that you shouldn't do something but you did it anyway and it turned out badly? Have you noticed sometimes when faced with an important decision that everything falls easily into place? Both are examples of how intuition can help guide us to the right path. You can't find that on the internet, in a book or through someone else. The answers about how to make decisions and handle your own life aren't "out there" somewhere. They exist inside of you.

Trust your own instincts. Trust your judgment. Trust yourself.

✦ ✦ ✦

Day 10

Every rosebush will bloom again

Today's message is about renewal. I live in the midwest, so we have four seasons here. Every fall, the leaves on the trees turn brilliant shades of crimson, orange and yellow before dying and falling to the ground. It's the end of a season, the end of a cycle—but certainly not the end.

Much like the leaves that will again become green and the flowers that will blossom through the warmer months, we are in a constant state of renewal. We may grow tired or weary, only to again find our inner strength. We may become ill, but will recover. We may cry over our losses, yet still find peace and the will to move forward.

Don't be too hard on yourself. Remember: Every ending is a new beginning.

+ + +

Day 11

Change your thoughts; change your life

When life gets us down, it's easy to get stuck in a negative thinking pattern. We tell ourselves things like: "I can't" and "I'm not good enough." Sometimes, we do this out of a fear of failure. Other times, it's because people have said these very phrases to us and we begin to believe them.

The truth is: You ARE good enough. You deserve happiness. You CAN and WILL accomplish your goals, if you believe in yourself.

Next time you catch yourself thinking something negative, try replacing those thoughts with positive ones like:

"I can do this."
"I am a worthwhile person."
"I deserve good things."

Then watch you life change before your eyes.

✦ ✦ ✦

Day 12

Don't turn a challenge into a trauma

Every person faces illness, disappointment, betrayal and hardship. It's a part of life. Why do some people seem to handle issues so well while others fall apart? The answer lies in the way they look at things.

You can focus on your misfortune, tell yourself it isn't fair and throw a full-blow pity party. Or you can reach inside yourself and pull out your inner strength, that light that burns within each of us and gives us the will to move forward. It's your choice.

Don't get me wrong: it's okay to be angry, sad, frustrated or disappointed when something bad happens. You have every right to feel however you need to feel. At some point though, you need to let go and move on.

Remember, a challenge—no matter how difficult—is an opportunity for growth. You can use it to rise above an obstacle rather than fall into the pits of despair. You have that power. Why not use it?

+ + +

Day 13

"Just keep swimming."
~ Dory, *Finding Nemo*

The ability to move forward despite obstacles is a crucial life skill.

In the Disney children's movie, *Finding Nemo*, Nemo's dad is feeling depressed because his son is missing, and he has no idea where to find him. Dory says these words to him:

"When life gets you down, you know what you gotta do? Just keep swimming."

This message is significant for many reasons. First, it suggests that we don't need to let anything hold us back. Second, it reminds us that we are strong and can get through challenges. Dory encouraged her friend to not give up and to keep moving forward.

I've done a lot of "swimming" in my own life lately. My family has faced many challenges, and I have been trying hard to keep things running as smoothly as possible. Some days I think if I pause for a moment to rest, I will sink to the bottom of the ocean and then what good will I be to everyone else? So I just keep swimming.

You may be feeling this way as well. Maybe you're overwhelmed. Perhaps you feel like quitting and giving up. Maybe you're afraid of what the future holds. These are the times we need to reach deep inside ourselves and find that inner strength we often forget is there. Most people doubt themselves and their ability to handle things. We wonder: "Am I strong enough to get through this?" The answer is: You are!

A little exercise I like to do when I'm feeling doubtful about my ability to handle life is to think of all the things I've already overcome. When you look back and remember the times you didn't believe you could do something but did, a pattern emerges. You'll see that no matter how difficult life got, you made it through. It may not have been easy, but you did it. And you can do it again!

+ + +

Day 14

Happiness is not a destination; it's a way of life

Many people say there are no coincidences in the universe, so when something jumps out at me, I take note. When I was in Ace Hardware one day, I found myself face-to-face with a wooden sign bearing this important reminder:

Happiness is not a destination; it's a way of life.

First, I'd like to say I'm guilty of not following this one. Like many people, I always seem to have some sort of plan or goal that I believe will make me happy. If only I could lose 20 pounds...if only I could land my dream job...if only I lived in a different house...if only I wasn't alone. The problem with this is you're putting your happiness on hold while you work to achieve something. Is being happy really supposed to be so much work? I think not.

Happiness is not a place or destination we need to get to. It's more of a mindset. If you notice, the people who are happiest are not necessarily those who are rich, thin, beautiful, successful or in a relationship. Instead, they are those who appreciate what they have and make a point to enjoy life. You don't need to go anywhere or do anything to be truly happy. Happiness is a choice you make. It's a lifestyle.

Today, I look around at all I am grateful for. I choose happiness. How about you?

✦ ✦ ✦

Day 15

Let your light shine

As sad as it is to admit, for a while I allowed life circumstances and negativity to block me from using my gifts. I stopped writing for a while, deactivated my website and wasn't helping others as much as I wanted to. I felt depleted and didn't believe I could be useful to anyone. The truth is: I wasn't allowing myself the opportunity to even try. So today I'd like to share an important lesson for us all: Don't allow other people or outside influences to dim the light you have inside of you.

I am and have always been a writer, teacher and helper. On good days and bad, that never changes. The only thing that does change is whether I'm willing to push through challenges to practice what usually comes naturally to me. And guess what? I've decided to make a bigger effort to do so.

Over the past several months, friends and family have asked me if I've written anything lately. One person (an awesome writer himself) urged me to get back to my work. He reminded me that writing doesn't come easily to most people and that I shouldn't let my talent go to waste. Another person—a stranger in pain—reached out to me via email to say an article I wrote a while back made her feel better. Clearly, I'm needed far more than I realized.

After making some much needed changes in my life, including moving to a new home, starting an exercise program and deciding I'm no longer willing to tolerate being mistreated, I returned to writing temporarily. I again used my gifts to help others in need. However, my light dimmed again while going through my divorce. I felt so helpless and hopeless and lonely that I couldn't find the motivation to write. I also feared my bleak mood would bring others down instead of lift them up, so I chose to stay silent for a while.

Although not fully healed yet, I'm in a much better place now. Once again, I am ready to shine my light to hopefully help others find their way.

Whatever your passion is, wherever your talents lie, do your best to share that with the world when you are able. People need hope and encouragement.

+ + +

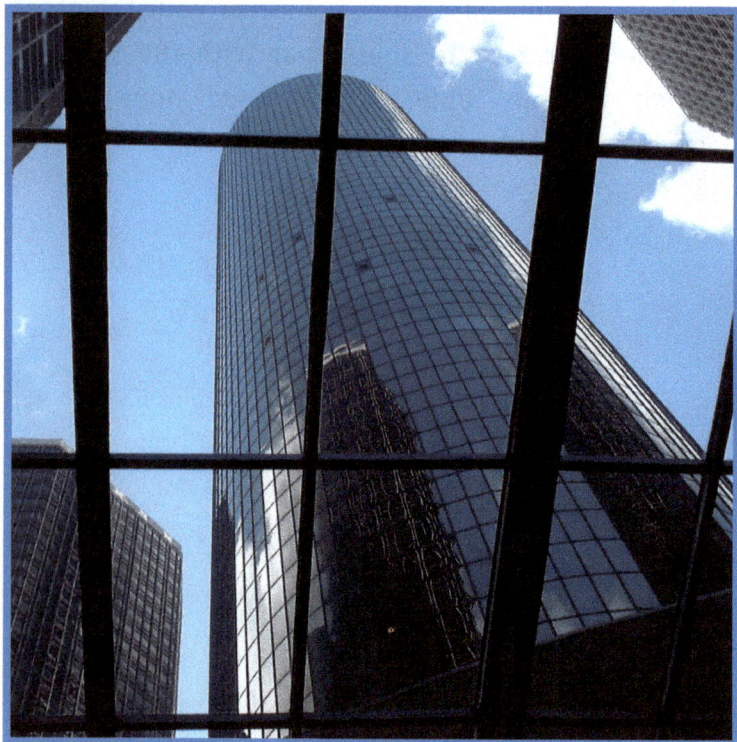

Day 16

Know your worth

We know the scenario all too well. It goes something like this: Someone criticizes you, gets angry, talks behind your back or betrays you, and you end up feeling bad about yourself. You may wonder what's wrong with you or blame yourself for their behavior. You may even feel unworthy of love. The problem with this is that we allow others to determine our value, rather than doing that for ourselves.

Of course, we all make mistakes; we're only human. But your mistakes shouldn't define you. They are an opportunity to learn and grow, not a reason to dislike yourself. Also, it's important to remember that many times when someone treats you badly, it has very little to do with you and is usually more about them and their own past trauma or insecurities.

Only you can determine your worth, so don't let others decide for you. Be the person you truly are, and those who are meant to be in your life will love you for you.

✦ ✦ ✦

Day 17

Live simply

Most of us wonder: how can I make my life better? How can I be happier? I'd like to share a little tip that has really helped me lately. It's based on the belief that "less is more."

I've spent a good portion of my life trying to figure out what makes me happy. Over the years, I've collected a lot of stuff and also ended up in a big house with a big yard. Although my family made some precious memories there, I realized as I became older that none of the material things really mattered. What counted most—and what made me happy—were the times spent with family and friends and out in nature.

As time went on, I actually started to stress about having too much stuff and too much house and yard to take care of. I believed these things took up a lot of my time and often interfered with my ability to relax, enjoy life and spend quality time with my family. After discussing these concerns with my then-husband and daughter, we all agreed that we not only needed a change, but we also needed to downsize our home and purge a bunch of our stuff. It was one of the best decisions we've ever made! We traded our 2,500 square-foot home for much smaller condo with a lot less things and no yard work. Finally, we were better able to focus on what really mattered.

If you find yourself bogged down by too much stuff, consider cleaning the clutter and donating items to charity. Do your best to get back to the basics and live simply. Remember what's most important in your life and try to do more of that. Your life will improve because of it.

+ + +

Day 18

What matters most?

What matters most? Twenty years ago, I read a book with this very title. It was designed to help figure out what's most important to you, so you could live your life more in line with your values.

I completed a series of exercises and discovered, not surprisingly, that my leading core values are: Family, Honesty, Compassion and Appreciation of Nature. I bring this up because I believe we're all doing this right now: trying to figure out what matters most to us. We're in a unique time of global self-reflection and discovery. The world is in crisis, and like it or not, we must adapt and find better ways of living that ensures not only our survival, but also our ability to grow and thrive. The pandemic caused us to look deep inside ourselves and re-evaluate our lives and our futures. What makes us happy? What gives us peace? What do we really want?

It's easy to lose sight of these things when we're so busy trying to earn a living, do what others expect us to do and achieve something we believe is meaningful. If there's anything the Covid-19 pandemic has taught me, it's to focus more on what matters most. I find myself really appreciating my family and friends and truly enjoying nature. I look forward to daily walks outside way more than I ever enjoyed shopping. Instead of striving to achieve a performance-based task, I get great satisfaction out of helping others—whether it's talking to a friend in need, texting pictures and nice notes to others, or offering a little surprise to brighten someone's day. I am no longer willing to tolerate negativity, disrespect or unkind words. Life is too precious for that.

Clearly a lot has changed, and our world may never be the same. Sometimes that scares me; other times I feel empowered. The future can be whatever we want it to be. We don't have to go back to living in a stressful, hectic, demanding world. Instead, we can take time to appreciate what matters most: the people and this beautiful planet we have been blessed with.

✦ ✦ ✦

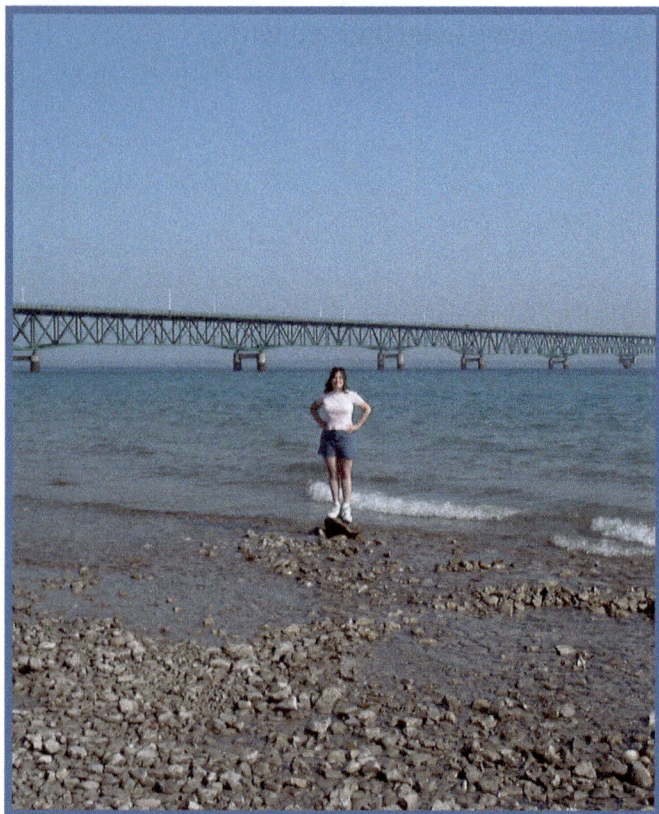

Day 19

You can!

I can't. It's probably the most self-defeating phrase in the English language. The minute you tell yourself you are unable to do something, you prevent yourself from doing it. You set yourself up for failure.

The very act of believing makes you able to achieve what you once thought was unachievable. So next time you have doubts about what you can do, remind yourself that your beliefs will make it happen—or not. It's all up to you.

✦ ✦ ✦

Day 20

Thinking won't solve your problems. Doing will

When we have a problem, it's natural to think about it and worry about it. Some of us, particularly those with anxiety, obsess or ruminate about our problems. But thinking alone won't result in a solution. To successfully deal with a problem or overcome a challenge, we need to take action.

I know from experience this is easier said than done. We may want to lose weight, but have trouble motivating ourselves to exercise or eat better. We may want reduce our stress levels, but don't make time for ourselves or give ourselves the break we need to do so. We may want to improve a relationship, but dwell on the negative or how things are broken rather than do what we can to make the relationship stronger.

In my own life, I've often neglected my needs in order to take care of everybody else and everything else. As a result, I felt stressed and would think: "I need to find some peace." "I need to decompress and recharge my tired batteries."

For a long time, I did nothing. Then finally, I went to a meditation class. I turned off my phone for an entire hour and let go. It was the best thing I did for myself in a really long time. Not only did I get the hour of stillness I needed, it also helped me to better handle life afterwards, to remain calmer and to more successfully give my family what they needed.

Why not give it a try? Stop thinking so much and take some action. Do something to take care of yourself for a change. Even a little baby step in the right direction can make a world of difference.

✦ ✦ ✦

Day 21

Stay positive. Stay strong

I've told myself these very words many times, and I believe everyone needs this reminder.

Whether dealing with health issues, relationship problems, losses or the everyday wear and tear of life, it's important to maintain a positive outlook. No matter what you're faced with, you can choose to confront it with hope.

Don't let sadness or worry overcome you. Keep moving forward and do all you can to live your life to the best of your ability.

✦ ✦ ✦

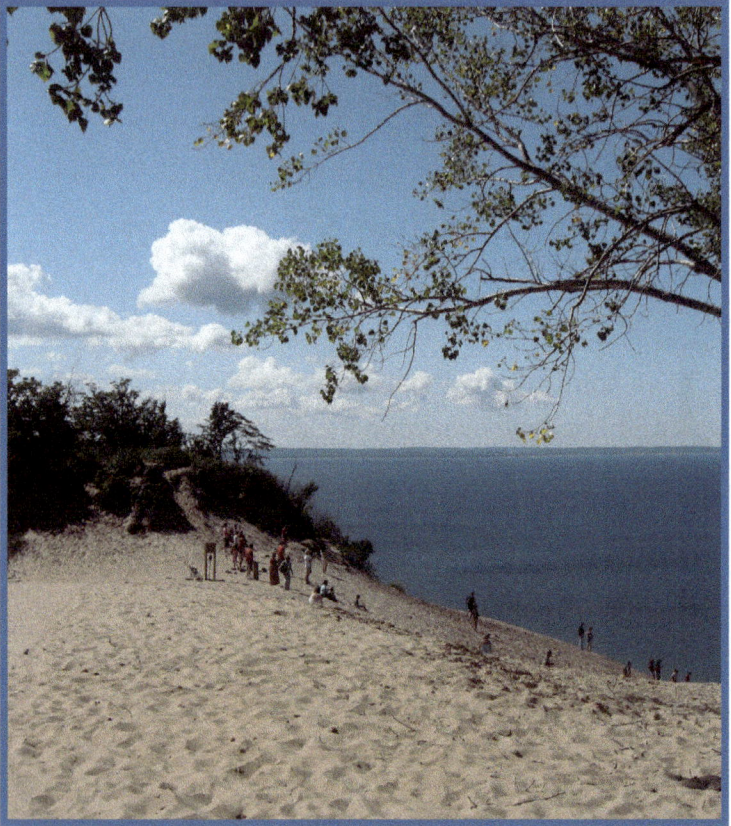

Day 22

Don't give your power away

The world is full of opinions and judgment. And since most of us care what people think, we often let others influence our choices and tell us who we should be. When we do that, we lose power over our own lives. We are no longer true to ourselves.

You are worthwhile and valuable, just as you are. Not everyone will agree with your choices, and that is okay. Don't allow other people control you or mold you to suit them. The only person who knows who you are, what you want and what you can achieve is you. Use your own power to create the life you want. You will be much happier for it.

✦ ✦ ✦

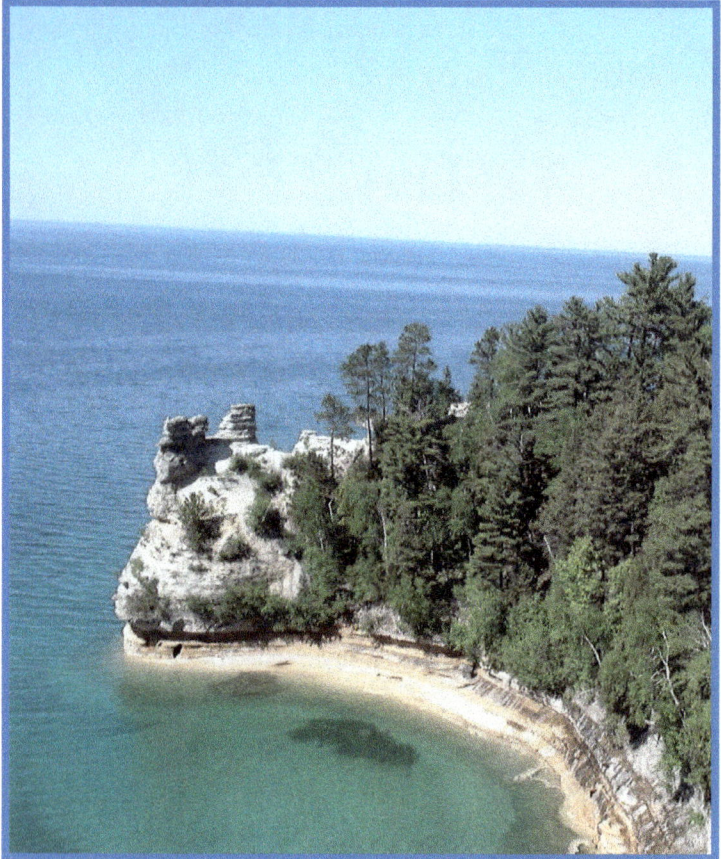

Day 23

When you follow your dreams, things eventually fall into place

Have you ever noticed when you don't pursue your passions or interests, life seems so much harder? I'll never forget a line I read from a book years ago that said: "Do what you love and the money will come."

Too often we get caught up in what we think we're "supposed" to do. Our life's choices are guided by what everyone else expects of us. I'll admit I'm a people-pleaser, so naturally I never want to let anyone down. But in the process, I sometimes let myself down.

Missed opportunities. Getting stuck in a rut. Feeling like life has no meaning. These are all the result of not pursuing your interests. Remember, if you are truly passionate about something, you will find a way to make it work.

It's time to do the thing you've always wanted to do.

✦ ✦ ✦

Day 24

Embrace this moment and find your inner peace

The world is a busy, hectic place. In the midst of the chaos, it's important to take some time to slow down.

Visit that place of stillness once in a while, that inner state where your problems seem far away and nothing else matters except here and now. You can do this in a variety of ways such as meditating, walking, spending time in nature, listening to music or sharing a special moment with your loved ones. Find what works for you. Take some time out to be peaceful and enjoy the present.

✦ ✦ ✦

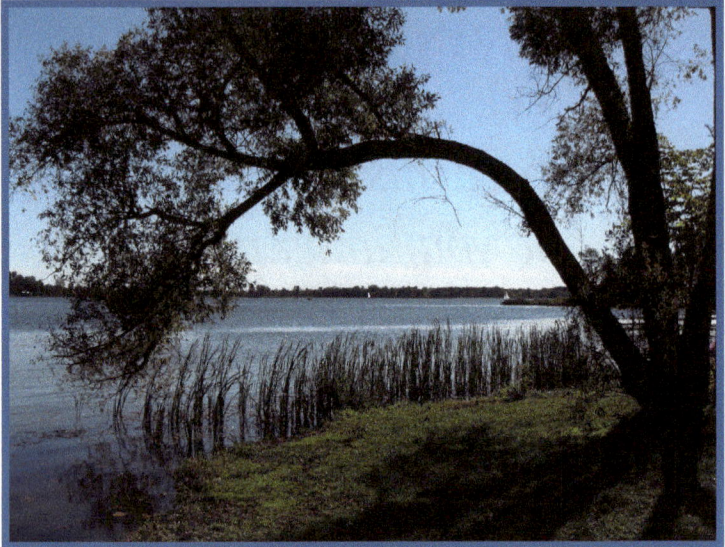

Day 25

Be thankful. Your gratitude will attract more positive experiences

This week's message is really simple: Count your blessings. Appreciate your family and friends. Give thanks for a good meal and time together with those you care about. Look around at all you have, rather than focusing on what's wrong or what you don't have. There is always something to be thankful for!

The very act of appreciating your life will draw positivity to you, which in turn will create more positive experiences.

✦ ✦ ✦

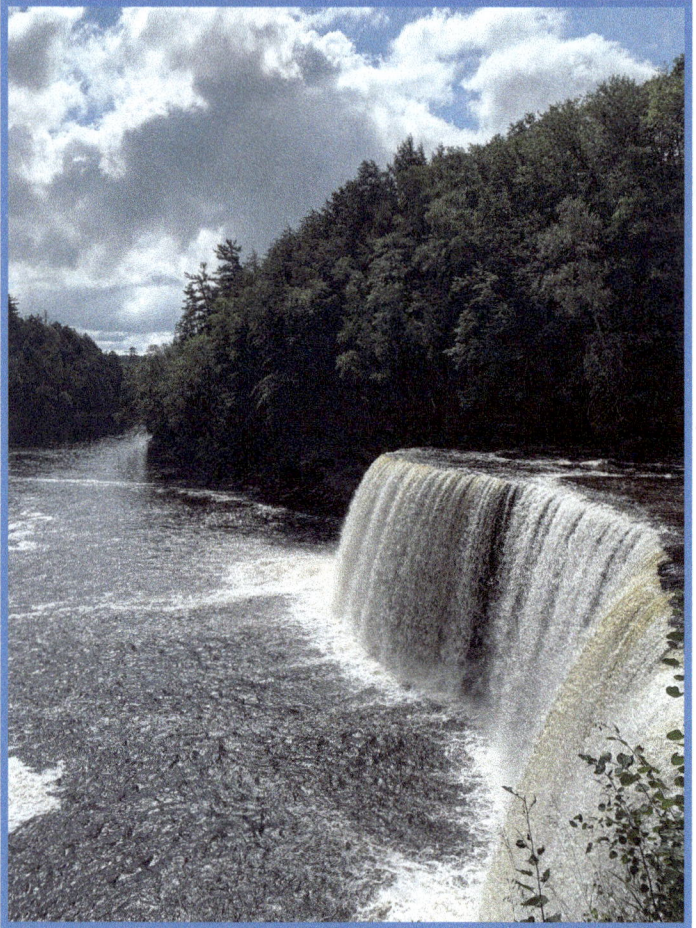

Day 26

Let it go. Release past hurts and live for now

You don't have to be a Disney princess to realize you don't need to hold on to that which no longer serves you. Anger, fear, resentment, guilt, past hurts and disappointments—you can let it all go.

Remember, you are not the same person you once were. Don't let the past cause needless suffering and keep you from fully enjoying life today. Let it go.

✢ ✢ ✢

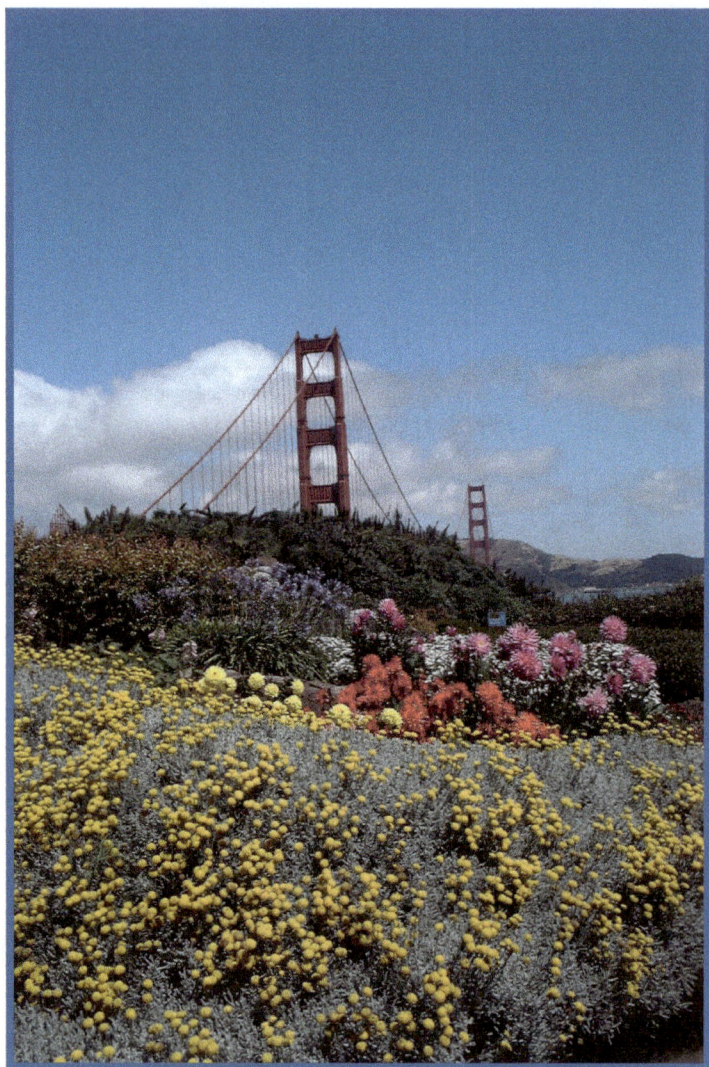

Day 27

You're only powerless if you think you are

I've talked about this topic already, but it's worth repeating. When you say "I can't," you automatically prevent yourself from achieving something.

My daughter and I saw *Robin Hood* at the theatre, and this very message was in the movie. (I love when movies offer tidbits of wisdom!) Robin was about to give up fighting for what he believed in. He felt he just couldn't do it. The task was too big. Then John said to him: "You're only powerless if you believe you're powerless." These words provided some much-needed reassurance and convinced him not to give up.

So if there's something you really want to accomplish, believe in yourself. Remind yourself you can do it—and chances are, you will.

✦ ✦ ✦

Day 28

Miracles are everywhere.
Take time to notice them

Christmas is the season for miracles—from celebrating the birth of Jesus to helping those less fortunate to reconnecting with loved ones near and far. But one important fact we often forget is miracles don't end when the holiday season is over.

Often we get so caught up in tragic news stories and negative comments that we overlook the good in the world. Yes, bad things can and do happen. That doesn't mean we need to let them take over our thoughts and our lives. Take a break from television and social media. Get out and look around. You'll find there is much kindness and plenty of positive energy for everyone. You'll see miraculous healings and people overcoming insurmountable obstacles and maybe even meet someone who is working hard to make a difference in others' lives.

Be sure to embrace the miracle of life and appreciate its beauty each and every day.

✦ ✦ ✦

Day 29

It's never to late to make a change

A New Year motivates us to do better and make positive changes in our lives. For many, this increase in drive often fades by the end of January, even though we may have good intentions.

If your New Year's resolution has fizzled out, there's no need to beat yourself up about it. No matter what day of the year it is, we can choose to take a different path, pursue a new interest or finally do the thing we have been putting off doing for so long. While change can be scary or uncomfortable, it is also empowering and can lead to a happier, healthier life.

✦ ✦ ✦

Day 30

Say what's in your heart

We're all guilty of sometimes not saying how we really feel because we're afraid of being judged or rejected. But holding back your feelings and not sharing what's in your heart doesn't actually protect you; it prevents you from making deep and lasting connections with others.

Solid relationships are formed by sharing the most vulnerable parts of ourselves—not just the good stuff, but our fears and pain as well. If you love someone, by all means, tell him or her. If you're afraid, admit it. If you're sad or hurt, don't pretend everything is okay. No one can ever know the real, authentic you if you don't let them in.

I remember when I wrote my first book, *From Pain to Parenthood*. I was afraid people would read it and think I was weak or crazy. But I knew I had some valuable insight to share that could help others who were facing similar life challenges. So I did it anyway. I put myself out there, not knowing what to expect. I let the world see the real me, not the one who smiles and says everything is fine when her heart is breaking. Not the one who refuses to admit her life is messy and imperfect. And guess what? Not once did anyone think I was weak or crazy. Instead, they saw strength and perseverance. By putting myself in a vulnerable position, I was able to make a difference in people's lives. And for that, I am truly grateful.

It turns out that saying what was in my heart—despite my fears and insecurities—was worth the risk! It can be for you also.

+ + +

Day 31

You're not a victim;
you're a survivor

An old friend and I were talking recently about our pasts. I brought up the abusive relationship I was in as a teenager and how after many years, I found a bit of peace with the situation.

"You're not a victim," she said.
"I know," I replied. "I'm a survivor."

After talking with her, I knew this was a great message to share. No matter what hardships or traumas you've experienced in your past, you are still here today. You're living. You're moving forward to the best of your ability. That says a lot.

So instead of thinking about how you were hurt, betrayed, traumatized or victimized, remember the strength and courage it took to get to today. You are a strong, capable person. You are a survivor!

✦ ✦ ✦

Day 32

Love is powerful and important. Handle with care

I spent a long time thinking about what to say about love. I truly believe love is the most powerful emotion we can ever experience. It can transform lives, bring great joy, heal illnesses and change the world. However, it must be nurtured and handled with great care and respect. Love is never something that should be taken lightly or disregarded. Like a flower that needs sunlight and water to thrive, love also needs nutrients to remain healthy and grow.

What I am hoping is that you think about those you love with the utmost gratitude and admiration. Remember why you love them and don't take your relationships for granted. Don't assume the other person knows what you're thinking or how you're feeling. Good communication is a key component of a healthy, satisfying relationship.

If you feel disconnected from your partner, it's time to talk things through. It's far better to have an uncomfortable or difficult conversation than run to someone else and ruin your relationship. Those feelings of hurt and betrayal are very hard to recover from.

And whatever you do, please be honest, trustworthy and respectful. Even the greatest love in the world can be tarnished when trust is lost or when someone doesn't feel valued.

If you love with your whole heart in good times and in bad, your life will be richer and more rewarding because of it.

✦ ✦ ✦

Day 33

Trust and let go

If you're a parent of a teenager, you know how tough the teen years can be. The drama, the mood swings, the attitude, the hormones...it can wreak havoc on not only the child but also his or her parents. It's a roller coaster of emotions, and you never know what you're going to deal with next.

One day when my daughter was 13, she became very angry with me. (Anger during the teen years is common, but this time was extra memorable.) She said I was annoying her, asking too many questions and invading her privacy. Of course, she has a right to privacy. I respect that. However, she was only 13, so when it came to things like internet use, school and relationships with friends, I felt I needed to check in from time to time to make sure everything was okay. Still, she gave me the attitude and the dreaded icy glare—and I felt bad.

That night, I questioned whether or not I handled the situation properly. I read articles about how other parents handle such things, trying to decide if I needed to change my approach. I was up during the night thinking and worrying because I don't want to ruin my relationship with my daughter or shatter her trust by being overprotective or invasive. I prayed for help in being a better parent and strengthening my bond with my daughter. After lots of worrying, I fell asleep with no solution.

The next morning, everything became clear. My daughter's mood had changed. She came into the den with a smile. She actually gave me two hugs, which is rare these days. I apologized for upsetting her, and she replied: "It's okay. You're just being a mom. I understand."

What? My angry child who acted like she despised me last night is now fine with my parenting choices? How could this be? Well, the answer is that she's a teenager—sometimes moody and hormonal, sometimes happy, and always trying to establish her independence and autonomy. It's what teens do. So instead of feeling bad and spending hours reading and stewing over the situation, I should have just let it be and trusted in my ability to make good choices for my child. Even when she's upset and would prefer I didn't do something, she still knows in her heart I'm a good mom and I always want what's best for her.

Next time you're faced with a problem and you're not sure if you made the right decision, don't stress about it. Just let it be and allow life to unfold the way it's meant to. Trust that everything will work out. Chances are, things will look much different in the morning.

+ + +

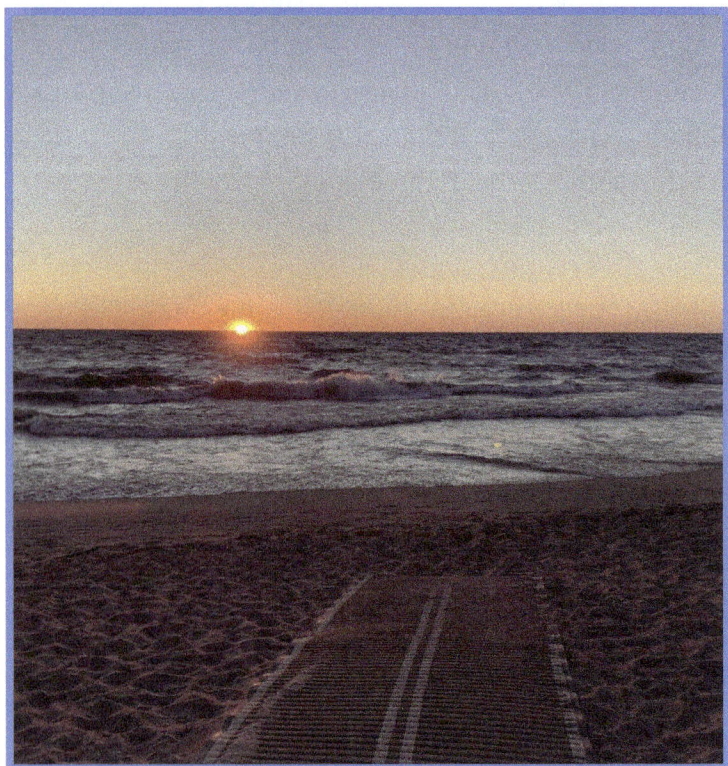

Day 34

Believe in yourself

How do you accomplish your goals? Is it through hard work and perseverance? Is it because you make smart choices? While all of these definitely contribute to your success, the single most important thing you can do is to believe in yourself.

I remember many years ago a friend told me I would never be a writer.

"Everyone wants to be a writer," he said. "It just doesn't happen."

Despite what he said, I knew I could do it. I believed with all my heart I would be a writer someday. So, right after college, I worked as a clerk for a pharmaceutical company while volunteering as a writer for their employee newsletter. Then I got a job in desktop publishing and offered to edit their training manuals. Next, I applied at a company I always wanted to work for and continued to apply for every job I was qualified for. Although this went on for an entire year, my hard work and perseverance paid off. I finally landed a job as a copy editor, which was a stepping stone to a full-time writing position. Four years after college, I became a professional writer.

My point is: when someone tells you that you can't do something, don't believe it. No one knows what you're capable of except you. Believe in yourself and chase those dreams, no matter how impossible they may seem. You can do it!

✦ ✦ ✦

Day 35

Better days are ahead

It's no secret I've had my share of struggles—my marriage, family relationships, parenting, health, my life's purpose. I often don't know where my life is headed, and that really scares me. I want to offer the world some positive advice and words of encouragement, but it's so difficult to do when you're feeling lost yourself. So, the best I can offer is to say that better days are ahead.

If you're struggling, like me, remember that life happens in cycles—good and bad, up and down, happy and sad. We all go through times in our lives where things are not going well. And then, one day, the cycle shifts and everything changes.

I pray that better days are soon ahead for everyone. May you find what you need, whether it's the strength to carry on, the wisdom to make the best choices, or the peace you seek.

✦ ✦ ✦

Day 36

Love never dies

Death is clearly one of the most difficult hardships we face. For those grieving the death of a loved one, I offer this message to you: Love never dies.

Not only do I believe this because our feelings and memories live on, but also because sometimes we are guided to do something that helps us cope. To illustrate, I'll share an example from my life.

One day, I felt compelled to read a poem I wrote for my grandfather after he passed. Ironically (or not), it was the anniversary of his death. I hadn't realized it until I looked at the poem and then noticed the date. When I saw it, I was more convinced than ever that I needed to share my story and this poem with others who are grieving.

My grandfather, who I called Papa, passed away when I was 29. I served as a pallbearer at his funeral, along with my sister. Right before we carried his casket, the funeral director allowed us a few minutes alone with Papa, during which time I lovingly placed a copy of the poem in his suit pocket so that he would carry it with him always.

I believe I was guided to read the poem on the anniversary of his death as a reminder that even when we are separated from our loved ones, love never dies. May you find comfort in these words:

THE FLIGHT OF THE EAGLE
by Deanna Kahler

The sun shone extra brightly that day
And all seemed right with the world
But it was time for the eagle to leave the place
That he called home
So as the grass became greener
And the flowers began to bloom
He spread his wings and let the gentle breeze
Lift him up into the sky

Although we will not see the eagle
In familiar surroundings again
He will always be with us in spirit
If you listen hard enough,
You can hear his whispers in the wind
If you watch closely,
You will see him soaring high above the earth
Looking down lovingly on all that he left behind

We may long to feel the tender brush of his wings on
our skin
But we don't need to reach out to feel his presence
For his love and kindness have touched us all
He has left a little part of himself
With everyone he has ever known
And all the hearts he has ever lifted

So next time you look up into the clouds
Know that he is there
Watching over us all
Seeing sights he had only dreamed of
And waiting until one day
When others will spread their wings and join him
In a paradise like no other

In Loving Memory of Papa (1920-1998)

✦ ✦ ✦

Day 37

"Death ends a life,
not a relationship."
~ Morrie Schwartz

In yesterday's message, I talked about how love never dies. While it's true we carry the memories and feelings we have for our loved ones who passed in our hearts and minds, I believe there is more to it than that.

My life experiences have shown me that not only is love alive in your heart, but it still exists in their spirit as well. Let me explain.

When I was in my twenties, my then-fiance (who now happens to be my ex-husband) decided he no longer wanted to get married and broke up with me. I was heartbroken. We had been planning our wedding. He proposed to me in Chicago on vacation and gave me a beautiful engagement ring. We had chosen a wedding date, picked out a hall and put a deposit on it. We had been dating for around six years and had what I believed to be a good relationship. The breakup came as a complete shock to me.

Afterwards, I had a lot of trouble eating and sleeping. I felt nauseous all the time. I cried a lot. It was a very difficult time. One morning after I had actually been sleeping, I awoke to the scent of my grandmother's perfume powder and thought I felt someone lying next to me. When I opened my eyes, no one was there. My grandma had passed away when I was 13. We were very close, and I believe she comforted me that day.

The experience brought me much-needed peace and reassurance. Plus, a few days later, Paul called me crying and wanted to see me. We ended up back together within a week and got married the following year.

That wasn't the only time something unusual

happened to me. In my forties, I found out a former boyfriend had passed away. I took his death harder than I expected. Even though I had moved on with my life and hadn't seen him in many years, I still had feelings for him.

His passing at such a young age left me feeling very sad and anxious, and I found myself thinking of him a lot. I went over our entire relationship in my head and felt guilty for not staying in touch with him or trying to be a part of his life in some way.

Not long after his death, I started hearing a song from his favorite band all the time. It was a song that reminded me most of him. Then, I heard a song he sang to me when we were dating. This was odd because it is not a song that is typically played on the radio these days, and I hadn't heard it played in decades.

I started to wonder if hearing these songs was more than coincidence, so I began talking aloud to him. During one of the "conversations," I said: "I don't know if you can hear me, but I just want to know that you're okay."

The next day, as I drove to a book signing, the car in front of me had a license plate that said:

I HEAR U

Chills ran down my spine. Coincidence? Maybe. I believed it was something more.

Several other unusual things happened in the months that followed his death. One day, I decided to test my theory that his spirit was actually reaching out to me. I spoke aloud to him again and said: "If this is really you, I want you to send me something. I want you to send me a pink rose."

A couple of weeks later, my family and I were up North and decided to have lunch at a park. I scanned my surroundings for a good place to eat our lunch and found a beautiful spot on the hill overlooking some trees. As I was about to sit down at the picnic table, something underneath my seat caught my eye. It was a fabric *pink rose*. Once again, I had goosebumps, and I knew the rose was meant for me.

The amazing experience in the park that day showed me that the people we care about don't just vanish from our lives when they die. A part of them lives on and watches over us. You may not see or hear them, but sometimes you can feel them. If you're lucky, they may even reach out to you in some way, whether as a bizarre coincidence, a song, a scent, an object or a lifelike dream. Even after death, our connections remain.

✦ ✦ ✦

Day 38

Don't let anyone destroy your inner peace

I've always been easily affected by other people's emotions. I can't help it; I'm empathic.

Throughout my life, this trait has been both a blessing and a curse. On one hand, I've been able to help people, which is awesome. However, I've also found myself feeling pretty awful after I've allowed someone to unload all their negative emotions onto me.

This is something many of us struggle with. We feel empathy for others and instead of just helping them and moving on, their pain becomes our pain. Their sadness becomes our sadness. It doesn't have to be this way. We can feel for people. We can reach out and offer words of encouragement and support, but we don't have to carry their burdens for them.

Today, I'm making a conscious effort to not let others destroy my peace. I encourage you to do the same. It's wonderful to care about people and offer to help. It's normal to feel sad for someone who is going through a difficult time. But being sucked into a web of negativity is not healthy or beneficial to anyone. Share your heart, but keep your peace. You deserve that.

+ + +

Day 39

Life is movement

Have you ever noticed when you're feeling down, the more you sit around thinking about it, the worse you feel?

One day, my then-husband and I were moping around the house feeling sorry for ourselves and our current situation. This went on for a couple of days until I decided I could no longer stay in that place. I got up one morning and refused to stay inside feeling bad. I told him that we were going to get out of the house and do something. We ended up at the local nursery choosing flowers to plant. When we returned home, I pulled weeds and planted the flowers, while my husband picked up sticks in the backyard. And guess what? We both felt so much better!

I believe there are two lessons to take away from this. One: nature is a proven mood lifter. When you're feeling sad or discouraged, try heading outside into the sunshine and fresh air. Maybe go for a walk or bike ride, head to a park, sit in the sun or do some gardening. You may not feel like doing any of this initially, but once you do, you will notice a positive difference in how you feel. Two: Doing any small task can break the cycle of negativity. Something as simple as picking flowers or walking down the street can take you away from the thoughts that drain you and keep you stuck.

Life is movement. Do your best to keep moving—no matter your situation—and you will notice your mood and your life will change for the better.

+ + +

Day 40

Don't run away from your emotions. It's okay to feel

Sadness is something we all feel but long to escape from. Sometimes, in an attempt to bury our pain or deny it exists, we keep our feelings hidden and suppress our emotions.

Such is the case with one of my loved ones. She is the type of person who keeps a lot inside and doesn't like to talk about her emotions. So, when faced with some sad news, her natural inclination was to remove herself from the situation, rather than confront her sadness. I encouraged her to stay.

"It's okay to feel sad. You don't have to run from your emotions," I said. "And you can even cry if you need to."

At first she was uncomfortable, but then she acknowledged her sorrow and began to cry. She got her emotions out, rather than keeping them bottled up inside of her. She released some of what she was feeling, which is healthy and cleansing.

No one wants to cry or feel sad. But it's a part of life. Emotions are what make us human. Allow yourself to feel whatever you need to feel. Give yourself permission to cry if you need to. You may believe crying is synonymous with weakness or think others don't want to be around you when you're sad, but neither is true. Being vulnerable takes strength, and most people will be very understanding and sympathetic when you're feeling sad. Plus, their kind words and actions may help you feel a little less alone.

✦ ✦ ✦

Day 41

We have a choice

I had been on a hiatus from writing when this phrase came to me. I was busy dealing with life's challenges and, quite honestly, it left me feeling sad and anxious.

My husband had been unemployed for almost 5 months. We were struggling with marriage problems, extended family conflicts, my husband's depression, the possibility of moving, my sister-in-law's declining health (she passed away from cancer in her mid-50s) and my usual worries about our daughter's well-being. The future seemed so uncertain, and that really scared me. I felt like I'd been given way more than I could handle.

At the time, I had a blog called *Weekly Wisdom,* where I would share encouraging messages, many of which are now found in this book. I felt guilty that I hadn't been keeping up with it. I wrote:

"Since I was a child, I've made it my life's mission to help others. But sadly I've been unable to do that lately. I've asked myself so many times: how can I possibly help others when I can barely help my family or myself? I've wanted to offer the world some words of comfort and hope, but for months nothing was coming to me. Until this morning."

You see, over the previous couple of days, family and friends had offered me *their* words of wisdom and encouragement. Some sent quotes or stories; others sent prayers. What they had in common were these important messages:

- Hang in there.

- Don't give up.

- You're not alone.

- Turn your problems over to God.

- Don't worry so much.

- This too shall pass.

All of these positive messages helped me to shift my thinking a bit. Then, that morning, it hit me: I may not be able to change what's happening in my life right now, but I do have a choice. We all have a choice. We can choose to put the past behind us and live for today. We can decide to not fear the future so much and remember that each day is a precious gift. We can be thankful for what we have right now, instead of being upset about what we've lost or how life isn't the way we want it to be.

Life may be hard, but the answer is simple. We all have a choice. Let's make it.

✦ ✦ ✦

Day 42

Share your home and your heart

While I was enjoying my backyard and its beautiful surroundings one sunny summer day, this thought popped into my head. *Share your home and your heart.*

Our homes are often our sanctuaries, our safe places. Sometimes we are leery of letting others in—both into our homes and our hearts— because doing so makes us feel vulnerable. We may worry we'll be judged or feel that someone may hurt us. But in order to fully experience life and love, we need to take that risk.

Don't shield yourself from the world in order to avoid future hurt or pain. Welcome friends and family into your safe place. Share your life and your dreams with others. Let them get to know the real you. Not everyone will like you, and that's okay. You will learn who fits into your life and who doesn't.

Most important, by sharing a part of yourself, you can make deeper and more lasting connections with others, which leads to a happier and more fulfilling life. And isn't that what we all want anyway?

+ + +

Day 43

Choose love

My message for today is sweet and simple: Choose love.

You may be thinking, why should I choose love when I've been hurt? Why should I be kind to someone who betrayed me?

The answer is: It is a healthier, more positive way of living. Hanging on to negative emotions can affect not only your health and well-being, but that of those around you. If you are mad or hateful, you will not be a positive influence on others. Plus, anger and hatred feels awful. It is not a good place to be.

Staying stuck in that mode deprives you of finding and forming loving relationships that can enrich your life and the lives of others.

If you have a choice between anger or forgiveness, choose forgiveness. If you have a choice between hope or despair, choose hope. If you have a choice between worry or acceptance, choose acceptance.

Life may not be easy, but we always have a choice. Make the one that brings peace and joy to you and those you care about. Choose love.

+ + +

Day 44

It's not yours to handle

These are the words that came to me one night as I sat quietly in prayer and reflection.

After having an emotional conversation with a loved one, I unplugged from the world for over an hour. My phone was off, and I resisted the urge to scroll though social media as a distraction. I thought a lot about the word "handle" and what it means.

Handle implies hanging onto something, like a bike handle. But what I, and many others, need to do is the exact opposite: let go.

I saw an image in my mind of myself as a teenager riding my bike no-handed with a boom box in my lap, as I turned corners effortlessly. How did I do that? How did I not fall?

The answer is trust. I trusted that I would be safe. I believed that I would not fall. Many of us don't do that now. We go through life believing things won't be okay unless we take action. We're afraid. I wasn't afraid back then.

What are we afraid of exactly? It's different for everyone, but the themes are often the same. We're afraid of failure and the unknown. In my case:

- I'm afraid of something bad happening to my daughter.

- I'm afraid of failing as a parent.

- I'm afraid of losing her.

- I'm afraid of death and being separated from loved ones.

- Sometimes, I'm even afraid of being afraid.

We all have fears and challenges in life. The problem is that when we focus on them too much and don't trust that everything will work out, we lose a part of ourselves. Remember, even in the midst of chaos, there is order. Everything will work out the way it's meant to.

✦ ✦ ✦

Day 45

Keep moving forward, even when it's hard

People ask me how I stay strong given all that's going on in my life. My strategy has always been to just keep going. Feel like crap? Just keep going. Having a bad day? Just keep going. Filled with anxiety? Distract yourself and then keep going. Don't feel like getting out of bed? Push yourself. Do it anyway. Just keep going.

I'm not saying this will be easy to do. It's a big struggle, for sure! But if you do what you can, when you can and continue moving forward, you will get through some excruciatingly tough times.

Martin Luther King Jr. had it right when he said these powerful words below. The way through any life challenge or hardship is to keep moving forward. Sending encouragement and strength to all!

"If you can't fly, then run. If you can't run, then walk. If you can't walk, then crawl. But whatever you do, you have to keep moving forward."

~ Martin Luther King Jr.

✦ ✦ ✦

Day 46

Unexpected thoughts often hold deep insight and truth

Have you ever had a sudden thought that seems to come out of nowhere? It might happen upon waking, in the middle of the night or when you're winding down for the evening. These seemingly random phrases that enter our minds often hold deep wisdom and truth. It's like someone whispers in your ear to steer you on the right path or help you realize something important about your life.

Maybe these are messages from God, designed to guide us or help us "wake up" and take action. Perhaps, they come from our subconscious mind as we finally figure out something we didn't realize before.

Whatever the source, if you suddenly have a thought that makes you stop in your tracks, you should listen. It just might change your life.

✦ ✦ ✦

Day 47

Seek the positive

I had a bit of a realization while attending my niece's New Year's Eve wedding. We spend way more time and energy thinking about what's wrong instead of what's right. As I was on the dance floor, I noticed how awesome I felt. It didn't matter that my divorce was final less than three weeks ago, that my daughter continues to struggle with mental health issues, that people I love have passed away, or that I lost someone I once considered a good friend. All that mattered was that moment.

I was surrounded by music, excitement, laughter and so much positive energy. That experience helped me remember who I was—and who I still am. I saw a glimpse of the person who has been missing lately because I've been too caught up in life's stresses. I didn't even realize I had lost a part of myself in the process.

The week before the wedding, I shared a story with my daughter of when I was a teenager and some of the things I did. She looked at me with surprise and said: "Mom, I didn't realize you were fun when you were younger! I don't think of you that way. I just think of you as mom."

Then, last night when I was dancing the night away with my daughter and other family members, she remarked how maybe I really am a "party girl" at heart. She saw me in action, having a good time. Apparently, this was something she hadn't witnessed in a long time.

The truth is: When we surround ourselves with positive energy and/or positive people, we feel really good. The reverse is also true. When we're around people who are depressed, negative, angry or upset, it can drain us. If you're like me, you may even find yourself absorbing their emotions and feeling them yourself.

I'm convinced the solution to having a good life is to seek out more positive and uplifting experiences. Working in an elementary school is one of the best decisions I have ever made. Every day, I am surrounded by kids who are excited and enthused. There is so much positive energy in that building, and I can't help but feel good too. The same is true of dancing at a joyful wedding or attending one of my daughter's exciting dance competitions or having a fun night out laughing with good friends.

Life can get very heavy sometimes, but by seeking out those experiences that create joy, we can find a better balance.

+ + +

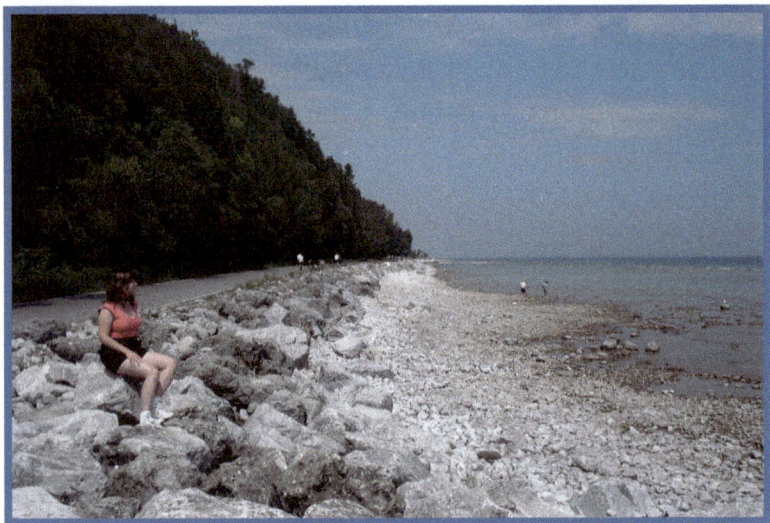

Day 48

You are enough

You *are* enough. Read that again because it's true. As someone who has spent most of my life feeling not good enough, I'm now learning to be ok with who I am. I hope you will too!

I've been given many labels in my life: shy, uptight, too serious, goody two shoes, too nice, dexter (as in poindexter), doormat, worry wart, too sensitive, etc. None of them made me feel good about myself. The worst one of all was when my then-husband told me: "You're almost what I want but not quite. Something's missing." Which I interpreted as "not good enough." This led me to think hard about what I was lacking and how I could measure up.

I spent years believing I needed to change for people to like and accept me, and I tried hard to be the person I thought everyone else wanted and needed me to be. And guess what? It didn't work.

Fifty years later, I'm still introverted. I feel awkward in social situations. My friends still describe me as sweet and really nice. I still have a lot of anxiety, although I've learned to manage it. No one calls me dex or dexter anymore, but I never lost my intelligence.

Have I improved in how I handle things? Yes, I have! Is it a little easier to be in social situations? Absolutely. I am not a different person than I was back then though. I'm the same me, only I've learned to function better. I'm finally learning to accept myself. Just because I'm not the best match for someone else doesn't mean I'm not good enough.

So please remember that when you doubt yourself or feel like you don't fit in. You are ok exactly as you are. You have your own unique personality, beliefs, interests and abilities. You have what it takes to be successful, to make a difference in the world and to make someone smile. You are loved. You are appreciated. Your existence matters. You are enough. Don't let anyone ever tell you otherwise.

+ + +

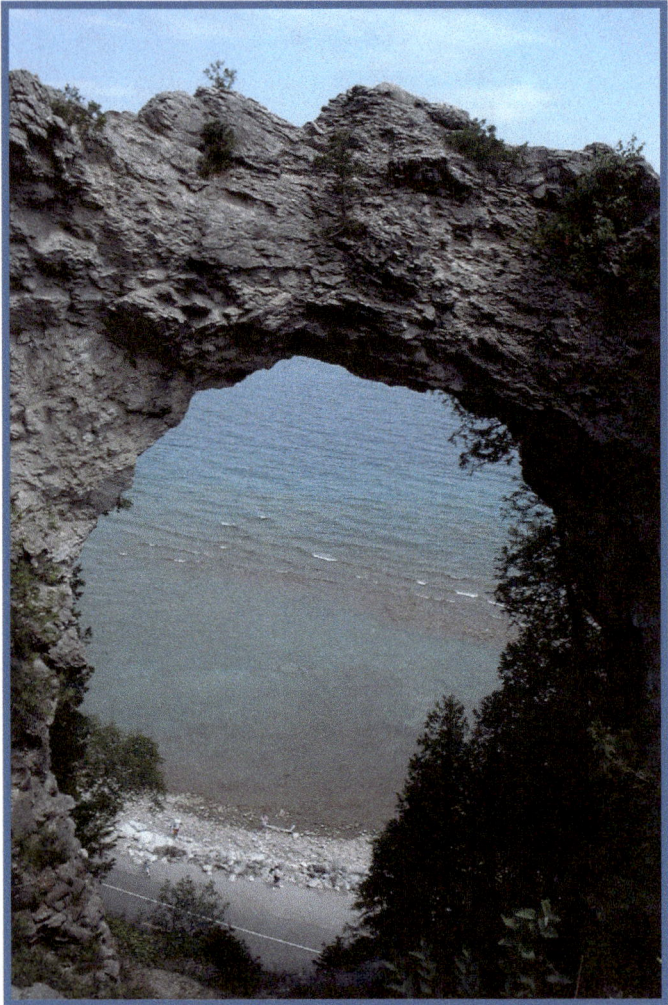

Day 49

It's okay to not be okay

*E*verything will be okay! I've heard this phrase a lot lately, and to be honest, it really started to bother me. It's natural to want to feel that life will get better. But expecting "everything" to one day be okay leads us to believe that if all is not perfect in our world, life cannot be good. And that's just not true.

I think it's healthier when going through a life crisis to acknowledge that everything doesn't have to be okay. We can still have good days and good moments in spite of our difficulties. We can plan for something and expect it to make our life better, only to learn it isn't what we want or need at all. This is something I've only recently come to realize in my adult life. Let me explain.

I spent years trying to land my dream job only to realize it was highly stressful and not well-suited to my personality. Tight deadlines, last-minute demands and a ton of work left me with daily headaches, rather than the sense of joy and fulfillment I thought I would feel. I can become easily overwhelmed when I have too much to do at once or when I don't have adequate time to complete a project or assignment properly. My career as a writer in the fast-paced world of advertising and publishing certainly didn't turn out the way I expected. But that was okay.

Another example is my road to parenthood. I expected to give birth to two children by the time I was 30 and have a "traditional" family. When I miscarried, I was devastated and didn't know if I would ever become a mom. However, that experience led me to adopt my amazing daughter. Was everything okay? No, it wasn't. My journey to become a mom was filled with heartbreak and sorrow. But that was okay. It was part of my life experience. And what I thought I wanted—to give birth and have a biological child —ended up not being what I needed at all.

The point is, sometimes we need to stop wanting everything to be ideal or perfect and accept that it isn't. Life doesn't always work out the way we plan. We may be faced with some pretty unfortunate circumstances. That doesn't mean we can't find happiness or joy.

Last summer, I traveled to Frankenmuth, Michigan, with co-workers to attend an early childhood conference. We laughed and giggled like teenagers. We drank wine on a riverboat cruise and went out to eat. We shopped and enjoyed the beautiful weather. It was a great couple of days!

When I returned home, I became very sad. The reality of my life hit me once again. I was going through a divorce, and the pain and grief of my situation weighed heavily on my mind and heart. Everything was not right in my world. But that was okay.

We can laugh in the morning and sob in the afternoon. We can have a great night with friends and feel depressed the next day. All of that is okay. It's all part of the human experience. So rather than hoping that one day everything will be alright, I am doing my best to recognize it doesn't have to be. Learn to be okay with not being okay.

✦ ✦ ✦

Day 50

I still believe

What can I say? Life is a bit of a mess these days. The entire world seems to be in crisis. There's more hatred, division, confusion and depression than I've ever witnessed in my life. When you add that to your own personal challenges and problems, life can be very overwhelming.

I'd be lying if I said I'm doing fine. Like many of you, my personal life is far from ideal. My divorce is now final, and I live alone half the time, which is very difficult. Family and friends who were once close have sadly drifted away. I hardly see or spend time with my sister anymore, and someone I once considered a good friend is no longer a part of my life. My teenage daughter is still struggling with her mental health, despite numerous attempts to find the best treatment for her. There's way too much drama! It's all so emotionally draining that I don't know how I survive some days. But I do. I'm still here plugging away, carrying the very heavy and important burden of taking care of everyone who needs me, while parenting, working, and managing a household, finances, activities and more.

How do I do this? The answer is: **I still believe**.

Despite the challenges life has thrown at me:

- I still believe in love.

- I still believe in the power of prayer to comfort, guide and heal.

- I still believe in the goodness in people and the world, no matter how many negative stories I hear or read.

- I still believe in honesty, trust, loyalty and commitment.

- I still believe that each one of us can and does make a difference, whether by lending a hand, offering a kind word or shoulder to cry on, or simply a smile.

- I still believe we can achieve our goals, even when they seem out of reach. I'm not one to give up easily and have always believed we can accomplish anything as long as we have faith and are willing to work hard for it.

- I still believe there are solutions to most problems, even when those problems seem insurmountable.

- I still believe there are better days ahead for all of us.

Plain and simple: I still believe. Losing hope just isn't an option for me. And I hope it won't be for you either.

+ + +

Day 51

Everything happens for a reason

Meant to be. Destiny. Fate. Many believe that the events and people in our lives are there for a reason. This makes sense when you think about how sometimes things just fall into place, and other times it's a big struggle to make something happen.

Have you ever been in a situation where everything that can go wrong does? Consider the possibility that you're not meant to be there. I know it's hard when you really want to make something work, even though you know it's not. This happens a lot with relationships. You love the person. You want to stay with him or her. However, no matter what you do, obstacles keep getting in the way. While it's true every healthy relationship requires work and communication from both parties, your life with your partner should not always be painful or difficult. When you no longer have many positive encounters, then it's time to move on.

I spent 34 years with the same person. We had many good times and happy memories. I don't regret marrying him and would do it all over again if given the chance. The last seven years of our relationship, however, were mostly miserable.

Negative events that had nothing to do with our marriage started happening. We had bats inside our home and spent thousands of dollars to get rid of them safely. My husband lost his job and was unemployed for an entire year, putting a strain on our finances and relationship. My daughter's room in the basement flooded, and we again spent thousands on new drywall, carpet and paint. Our air conditioning unit broke, again costing thousands. I started to notice that when my husband wasn't home, I felt lighter and more peaceful—definitely not a good sign! When you feel better when your partner is absent, that's a pretty good indication that your relationship is no longer beneficial to you. If you believe in fate, our struggles and conflict could be viewed as a sign that we were no longer meant to be together.

The mentality that everything happens for a reason and some things are "meant to be" doesn't just apply to relationships though. Take, for example, my journey to parenthood. I dreamed of becoming a mom since I was a little girl. I expected to have two children, one girl and one boy, by the time I was 30. However, life had other plans for me. I suffered two miscarriages and was ultimately led to adopt. Although losing two babies was devastating, everything fell into place with the adoption and just 9 days before my 37th birthday, we held our beautiful baby girl. She adjusted quickly and easily to our home and family. I couldn't love her more if she were born to me.

I'm sharing these stories to help reassure you that when things don't go your way, something else is waiting for you. You will end up exactly where you are meant to be.

+ + +

Day 52

The future is a blank canvas

An artist puts his brush to a blank canvas and creates whatever he wants or imagines. He realizes that if he doesn't like how his painting turns out, he can always start again with a fresh canvas or a coat of white paint. You can do the same with your life.

It's very freeing when you think about it. You may not like where you're at right now, but you don't have to stay there. You can create whatever kind of life you desire, one stroke at a time.

Do you want a new job? Are you hoping for a new relationship? Have you always dreamed of moving to a warmer climate? Then, do it! Pick up your brush and paint the life you envision.

I know, you're probably thinking, "But I can't." For whatever reason, you see obstacles instead of opportunities. We all do. No one likes to make a big change or take a risk. It's far less scary to stick with the familiar. But by doing that, you miss out on what could be. You lose the chance to make your life better, richer, more rewarding.

While I was going through my divorce, I had no idea where my life was headed. The truth is, I still don't. Although scary, I made a couple of changes that I suspected would put me in a better position. First, I left my job at a private preschool and church to work in a large public school district. It turned out to be a great move for me. The environment is so energizing, and I have more autonomy to make choices for my classroom and students. It was a difficult decision, but I'm glad I trusted my instincts. I'm in a place that is better suited to my working style and personality.

Next, I applied and got accepted to graduate school to earn my Master's degree and become certified to teach elementary school, rather than just preschool. This plan, if I follow through with it, will help secure my future as a single person. I will double or triple my ridiculously low income, have a better retirement plan and also receive full benefits. When my spousal support runs out, I will be able to not only pay my bills but also save money for the future.

Of course, this plan is not written in stone. I know anything could happen in the next couple of years. Regardless, I put a few fresh strokes on my blank canvas and will see where it leads.

You can do the same. If you're not content with where you're at, even making a few small changes can affect your future. So why not apply for a new job or go back to school or research a new place to live? Or maybe just take a cool vacation somewhere you've always wanted to visit.

The future can be whatever you want it to be.

✦ ✦ ✦

"Just do the best you can. No one can do more than that."
~ *John Wooden*

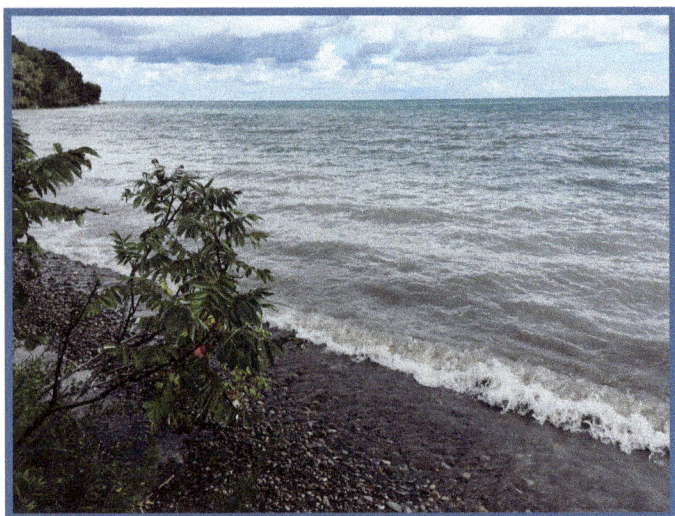

AFFIRMATIONS

- Healing takes time.
- The human soul is unbreakable.
- Your joy is on the other side of pain.
- Help is never far away.
- This too shall pass.
- Embrace the calm amid the chaos.
- Life is what happens while we're making other plans.
- Sometimes you have to just wing it.
- The answers you seek are within.
- Every rosebush will bloom again.
- Change your thoughts; change your life.
- Don't turn a challenge into a trauma.
- Just keep swimming.
- Happiness is not a destination; it's a way of life.
- Let your light shine.
- Know your worth.
- Live simply.
- What matters most?
- You can!
- Thinking won't solve your problems. Doing will.
- Stay positive; stay strong.

- Don't give your power away.
- When you follow your dreams, things eventually fall into place.
- Embrace this moment and find your inner peace.
- Be thankful. Your gratitude is like a magnet.
- Let it go. Release past hurts and live for now.
- You're only powerless if you think you are.
- Miracles are everywhere. Take time to notice them.
- It's never too late to make a change.
- Say what's in your heart.
- You're not a victim; you're a survivor.
- Love is powerful and important. Handle with care.
- Trust and let go.
- Believe in yourself.
- Better days are ahead.
- Love never dies.
- Death ends a life, not a relationship.
- Don't let anyone destroy your peace.
- Life is movement.
- Don't run away from your emotions. It's okay to feel.
- We have a choice.
- Share your home and your heart.

- Choose love.
- It's not yours to handle.
- Keep moving forward, even when it's hard.
- Unexpected thoughts often hold deep insight and truth.
- Seek the positive.
- You are enough.
- It's okay to not be okay.
- I still believe.
- Everything happens for a reason.
- The future is a blank canvas.

ABOUT THE AUTHOR

An empath and writer since childhood, award-winning author Deanna Kahler has made it her life's mission to help others. She has worked professionally as a writer and editor for more than 20 years and wrote her first book, *From Pain to Parenthood: A Journey From Miscarriage Through Adoption* in 2013. Since then, Deanna has authored many books, both fiction and non-fiction with the goal of helping to encourage and inspire people. Her titles are available on amazon.com.

In her spare time, Deanna enjoys walking, bike riding, dancing, visiting parks and spending time with family and friends.

For more info about the author, please visit www.deannakahler.com.

www.ingramcontent.com/pod-product-compliance
Lightning Source LLC
Chambersburg PA
CBHW051811090426
42738CB00032B/3035